MW00618169

"I don't drink," declares the spe(*Disguises*, but that speaker, an(beautiful collection, is word-drunk—world-drunk, entranced with the gorgeous world, its excesses, verbal, sensory, sonic, tactile. The book never stumbles in all its riot and plenitude: its artist-impresaria is tart-tongued, clear-eyed, and its observations sometimes sting.

The sheer array of prismatic assemblages in these poems does not, however, disallow a deep tenderness for the human gesture, the prayers and rituals that provide a momentary well of lifegiving water: at a petroglyph site, the speaker in "All Things" imagines the ancient artist using her materials "to touch me / across this sandstone, / my hand print over / her hand print."

This book is a map, to guide one to one's wildest, truest self.

—**Lisa Bickmore**
Utah Poet Laureate,
winner of Utah Arts Council Poetry Award
and the Ballymaloe International Poetry Prize,
author of *Haste and flicker*, and founder
of Lightscatter Press

"I pluck a buttercup growing / above your mortal / heart to press in my journal." That's Susan Elizabeth Howe at the grave of Emily Dickinson, whose ravenous intelligence and restless spirit would have delighted in the poems in *Infinite Disguises*. Howe's subject matter is vast and quirky, strange and wonderful, utterly beguiling. She is protean, by turns elegiac, hilarious, lyrical, wildly unpredictable. Nothing is beneath her notice. Whether speaking in the voice of a young cormorant, or paying homage to a potato, she dazzles in her disguises. One of the freshest, strangest, most terrific books I've read in a very long time.

—**George Bilgere**
author of *Central Air* and seven other poetry collections, Witter Bynner Fellow of the Library of Congress, and professor at John Carroll University

In her introductory poem, Susan Howe invites readers to join in the "pleasure and play" of *Infinite Disguises*. Meet a meth child, Sulis Minerva, Della Street, and buckle up while Jesus drives a convertible. Her imagination runs wild, roller-coasting with witty, contemporary language through diverse and timely topics. She weaves this wonderful collection with inspiration from Emily Dickinson. Howe raises an eyebrow to America's gods of money and self.

Yet, *Infinite Disguises* holds at its earth-loving heart, "the worm's quiet praise."

—**Marilyn Bushman-Carlton**
author of *on keeping things small*, *Cheat Grass*, and *Her Side of It*; Utah State Poetry Society Poet of the Year; recipient of the 2010 Award for Poetry from the Association of Mormon Letters

Infinite Disguises

BY COMMON CONSENT PRESS is a non-profit publisher dedicated to producing affordable, high-quality books that help define and shape the Latter-day Saint experience. BCC Press publishes books that address all aspects of Mormon life. Our mission includes finding manuscripts that will contribute to the lives of thoughtful Latter-day Saints, mentoring authors and nurturing projects to completion, and distributing important books to the Mormon audience at the lowest possible cost.

Susan Elizabeth Howe

Infinite Disguises

BCC PRESS

Infinite Disguises
Copyright © 2023 by Susan Elizabeth Howe

All rights reserved. Printed in the United States of America. No part
of this book may be used or reproduced in any manner whatsoever
without written permission except in the case of brief quotations
embodied in critical articles or reviews.

For information contact
By Common Consent Press
4900 Penrose Dr.
Newburgh, IN 47630

Cover design: D Christian Harrison
Book design: Andrew Heiss

www.bccpress.org

ISBN-13: 978-1-948218-90-0

10 9 8 7 6 5 4 3 2 1

To our sweet pug Chloe (2005–2018),
waiting on the other side of the rainbow bridge.

If we somehow look like our dogs,
I hope my spirit is as bright as Chloe's.

Contents

"I dwell in Possibility—"
              —Emily Dickinson

"She couldn't remember when she'd
had such room for being."
              —Barbara Kingsolver

Poem in Which I Try Not to Lie

"Tell the truth, but tell it slant," said Emily.
The very act of indenting a single space, pausing
 a hair's breadth, poses a question: what am I
  hiding in that hesitation, that momentary recon-
   sideration? Let's say a poem is a shimmery swimsuit
   I design. That's metaphor, imaginative, not exact
   truth. A poem is words arranged in lines to sing,
    if by sing I mean link in patterns aural, spacial, visual.
   But abstractions remove me from what I want
    to fashion, which is something to make you remember
    and wonder. So far that's only the swimsuit—
     an aqua and grape tankini? lightning-striped trunks?
     You'd better put on coconut sunblock and get under
     this airy gazebo to keep cool, relax on the orange
      and fuchsia flowery chaises longues near the pool
       where the entire volleyball team has gathered
        for burgers and brats to celebrate their Olympic
        victory. Well—I must be hosting the Brazilian men
         or the Chinese women. You see what happens?
         I do not consciously shift, my imagination pulls.
         And over time, the gap stretches and reveals itself.
         Both the Chinese and Brazilians have shown up,
          attracted to each other in their sexy swimwear, pairing off,
           splashing around in the deep end, using looks, gestures,
           a little English to communicate. Now through the gate
            come their friends with the drinks, and I turn on a mix
            of bossa nova and Chinese hip-hop and hope
             I've got enough of a spread to feed them all. Yes,
             I left the literal back by the title, but I welcome you,
              dear reader, to the party and invite you to join in
              the pleasure, the play, to take your own dive
               into what might be possible.

Hinges

To the Venerable Stars and Galaxies

We who are about to die salute you, about to die
from your expansive speeding-debris-from-the-big-bang
frame of reference, though in our own sub-sub-cosmic
solar and lunar systems, it seems to us we as a species
will be around for eons and generations. I admit I speak
only for myself, other representatives of my kind engaged
in checking electronic devices, whitening their teeth,
or curing insomnia. Lacking charisma, I suffer, famished
for love, and apologize for addressing your vast essences
in these little linguistic explosions, these minuscule vectors
of thought. My thesis statement is "find your dots,"
another diminution of your immensity, your indifference
to Earth and its species. You might respond, from impossible
distance, *Blow the block. Weed the jungle,* as I,
aware of the inter-textuality of literatures across time
and space, translate your impulses. But have I
arrived at your meaning? *What's the beta?* you ask;
my answer hinges between fish and particle. I need
to lighten up, as we say, to boil until my skin
hangs loose, which might account for my animus.
It isn't going to bleed is what I'm hoping, and
knowing there is no non-inertial frame of reference,
I beg you to beam your reply across the eternities:
Have you crunched the coordinates? Do you find me janky?

Susan Elizabeth Howe

Moon Cruise

Day One: Leaving port, thunderclouds ballooning in the distance, you will feel yourself expanding but will not yet know whether the mystery is within you or the cosmos.

Day Two: At sea. As the night lengthens, the captain will steer along the path set down on the water by the moon. You will sleep deeply and dream of extinct animals: their snuffling for food, their suffering, their private languages, their mating rituals. Each species will lodge itself in your body.

Day Three: In port at the famous Western Isle. If you dare, you can tour the underground caverns where so many have lost themselves in lava tubes and tunnels, but where others have found emerald caves, veins of silver, seams of salt. Spelunking gear and moon lamps will be issued on the promenade deck. Be warned: the ship departs at midnight and won't wait.

Day Four: We sail through the Lost Fjords and Glacier Alley, where we will pass five glaciers, translucent as the day moon, each of them receding. You may experience them as metaphors for your life. The glacier in Blizzard Bay will moan and clench, calving thunderous icebergs that will, like thoughts, flow through the world's currents or eddy in the doldrums.

Day Five: At sea. Distract yourself all day with art, gems, exquisite food, and beauty rituals, but you will know your body is floating into the deepest hole of the widest ocean, a void left by the moon's escape then filled with rushing salt water. On deck at midnight, you will look through enormous telescopes and feel the full moon resist any label you may impose: red, dark, dark red, shadowed—smoky body beyond your need to give in to its pull.

Day Six: We will dock on the new peninsula and tender in.
Will you, moon-fazed, moon-faced, be pulled into particles
and waves? Rise through blackness on reflected light,
lured by gravity other than the earth's? Escape your human
limitations or lose yourself within them? Who can tell?

Day Seven: Back at home port, you will disembark having
found, in the circle of your life, the moon's Seas of Cold, of
Showers, of Serenity, of Fecundity, of Nectar.

The Tenants of Philosophy

> *"Dickinson studied the tenants*
> *of Emerson's Transcendentalism"*
> —student paper

I try to explain various tenets, but some students
insist they are tenants and occupy all floors

of the great edifice of philosophy. The students,
so certain, must live in the neighborhood, frequent

the same bistros, laundromats, tanning salons.
They want me to know that Nihilist tenants

tend to offend Christians, paint their ceilings black,
project images of animal dissections on their living

room walls. Idealist tenants justify question-
able behavior thus: *A broken pipe in the mind gushing*

a gallon a second is far more destructive of lower floors
than the blown pipe in our kitchen, or *Hip hop at three a.m.*

is a weak echo of hip hop's perfect abstraction. And given
the subjectivity of observation, Skeptic tenants shift

appearances—now bearded skateboarder, pants waist
dipping below the butt crack, now filmy waif of a ballerina.

Which tenants embrace Audi TT's, Blend-Tech Blenders, Gucci
watches, all things material? Which insist reality is experiential?

These Transcendentalist tenants my student knows, I hope
to be introduced, to meet them for lunch at J-Dawg's.

I want the god in me to commune with the gods
in them. I want to talk solipsism and take selfies

to show my colleagues, the tenants laughing at my wit.
Or we'll all crowd into a booth and the student

who introduced us can snap the shot, establishing
Facebook proof the spirit speaks through many mediums.

Susan Elizabeth Howe

Answering Springsteen

> "What happens when all the things you believe in
> when you're 25 don't work?"
> —Bruce Springsteen

You spit out your venom. You lick
honeycomb, pollen, nectar.

You rent earth-moving equipment,
bulldoze walls,
scrape rubble into dump trucks.

You undergo a radical
splenectomy to get rid
of your spleen. You invite
desire back into your body.

You buzz like a hummingbird.
Hum like a bumblebee.

You plug yourself
into your instrument, splitting
all your molecules
into particles and waves.

You study fans like ants
after their hill washes out,
notice how they attach
to each other, dig out
one sand grain at a time,
taste and link
in search of the one queen.

You consider a healthier role
for the king.

The Case of the Jilted Jockey

Perry Mason, you are plot only
and the bug eyes of Raymond Burr.
Flat as asphalt on the Pasadena
Freeway. So is Della Street
disguised as your secretary asking
oh, Perry, how did you figure it out?
when she's been to law school
passed the bar practiced criminal law
on the side her secret all those years
you two ate lunch ate late swayed
in a houseboat overnight
drove along sea coasts slow danced
on an ocean liner from Vancouver.
The episode in which you and Della
act on your attraction? Not one
Erle Stanley Gardner will ever write.
He wants you all celluloid no passion
so skip the horse race slip off
for the afternoon wander
the labyrinths of Hearst Castle
while Bright Magic loses drugged
of course by that rat Johnny Starr
who deserves to be dead yes shot.
Did Tic throw the race he was fired
his wife left him for Johnny
of course the police grab Tic.
When do you get vacation days? Never.
So tell Paul Drake, "Shuffle the evidence
leave eerie notes expose the corruption
I'm taking Della to NYC *Flower Drum
Song* on Broadway and Buddy Holly

Susan Elizabeth Howe

on the *Ed Sullivan Show*." Next week
in court you'll nail the blackmailer
question Lieutenant Tragg the horse owner
the cheating wife name the killer
without any plausible clues bully him
into confessing who needs proof
the murderers act like cowed idiots.
Johnny's own stable hand did it,
not Tic. Time to decompress: none.
Gardner puts you right back
to work on the case of the perjured
parrot the terrified typist the vagabond
vixen the cautious coquette alliterating
his way through your fictional life.
Sneak off with Della take the convertible
he won't have a clue you're out
of his control sharing spicy tacos
fireworks the ferris wheel
on the Santa Monica pier
kissing off-camera dreaming up
your new firm Mason & Street.

A Malaise

feels like a phone call you pick up
before you notice it's from an area code
you don't recognize and the emotive
guy on the line says, *"Hello are you having
a pleasant day?"* when anyone local
would ask how's it going and it seems
this caller would be happier speaking Farsi
or Quechua, so he might say with more gusto
congratulations you've been selected
to participate in an important survey
about your satisfaction with the new *bin-dah*
(binder? blender? bender?)
you recently purchased online (I did?)
and if you'll only respond
to fifty simple questions the company
will contribute a thousand dollars
to saving the walrus or did he say
sieving the wool rust
and either you'll hang up
and show yourself to be the arrogant
dismissive warthog you try not to be
or you'll spend an hour on the phone stuck
with your general angst that maybe
the blue marble planet wants to roll over you,
maybe not, but it fills your life with problems
like why do you feel dizzy climbing this tiny
footstool and are your deepest convictions
merely electric impulses in a brain lobe,
convoluted questions like those the caller
is asking, questions you can't possibly
answer because you don't understand.

Susan Elizabeth Howe

Coup de Foudre

Out in the boat in the lightning
  your hair is standing straight up
    all over your head, my sister said,
      and I thought ball lightning bead lightning
        forked dry heat ribbon rocket sheet
          lightning and the buzzing
            of the boat hook and the sizzle.

The strike felt like
      being machine gunned
          in a gang fight, or,
      at the blackjack table, losing my last
          hundred bucks,

searing pain that entered
  maybe my ear in ten thousand volts
      and jolted my nerves spinal cord brain nerves
        and the air tasted metallic
as I began to come to
on my back.

In the hospital, I read
about survivors, nine out of ten, and some
claim along with intense pain
clairvoyance—precisely. Which is how I know

  my sister's husband wants me
  he saved me mouth
  to mouth she's wracked—afraid
  he'll leave her for my lightning

Why else would she thrust herself
between us and keep telling me
my mind's been charged discharged by

hot and cold air masses colliding
negative leaders meeting positive leaders
yes intense sensation for microseconds
but now only fragmented
patches of glowing gas.

||

The Writhing Animal

To My Unhappy Muse

You never honor me with poems.
No dreams, no visions. Ungracious, given
that I chose *you*, not some moist

filmy female. You, a primitive carved eagle,
a burn on your wing and a knot hole
in your tail. A snake in your mouth.
If I build a you golden perch
hung from chains in the ceiling,
wide enough for your formidable

wings to unfold and lift you
to the heights, will you fly out
sharp-shinned, hollow-boned,

and seize the most dangerous prey
of the visible and invisible worlds?
If not I'll leave you dangling

by your head from the bookcase
in the corner, scratching up spider legs,
dust mites, wings of web-trapped flies.

For years you have carried that snake
in your mouth, blood on your bitten breast.
I require a better compact. Stretch

out your neck, mouth wide,
promise. Drop the snake
into my throat, all fangs

and gemmed skin, the animal within
for my grappling. The writhing animal.

Susan Elizabeth Howe

"A Rush of Cochineal"

—Emily Dickinson

A hummingbird flew through her garden. At once
    she conjured a green Colombian gem,
        picked up a letter Shakespeare mailed

from the African coast through tempests
    imagined and real, and brushed the air
        with *cochineal*, dye in the crimson-scarlet spectrum.

The *ch* ought to sound like *sh*, sustained whisper
    of ocean or lush. But the word rhymes instead
        with *Gotcha, heel!*, an exclamation

one might address to a trapped thief.
    Not that Emily would call someone a heel,
        but I wonder if she knew in choosing

'cochineal' she also named the dye's
    source: desert insect, tiny female beetle
        that settles on a cactus and covers itself

in white froth, camouflage
    and crust, then lives on the toughness
        around the prickly pear's spikes. Harvesters

scrape them off with a deer tail.
    Crush one in your palm and juice red
        as suffering stains your calloused

hand. What is 'cochineal' after all
    but a way of seeing—meaning grasped
        through pulp, flesh, and needle?

She must have known the insect,
    not just the dye, despite living only
        where benevolent showers filled her

rain barrel. Her poems put away
    in a drawer, she must often have wandered
        the desert of bitter and little.

Susan Elizabeth Howe

Bathing My Mother

She thinks she is the princess
beloved of the castle and how
impertinent of me to mention her bath.

She thinks lights glitter
over her dinner from a reflecting ball.
Soon she'll waltz out
of her wheelchair. She only sits
to gather her breath, to sip
peach punch, to sparkle.

Of course I am jealous
or I would see her in silver
silk and a lavender sequined
sash. She is shimmer and plunge,
I am an old robe throwing
myself across her loveliness.

She thinks my plan
is to grab her, stash her
in a tub, numb her
in cold water a thousand years.
She hangs on to her arms, kicks
high and fast, calls me a wicked
crone, hideous.

She will never consent
to the stripping, the spray.
No, she will cut off
her hands and heels first,
leap bleeding into the well
and wait for the prince
to pull her out
of the drowning.

The Catechism of Toni Pardoe Ellsworth

in her own words

Q. *Who made you?*
My first job was Service Station Attendant

Q. *What else did God make?*
Gas 25 cents a gallon and the attendant pumped,
washed the windshield, checked the oil,
air, and wipers

Q. *Does God love you?*
I have been a Dental Assistant
Department Manager for Women's Shoes

Q. *Where is God?*
Diamonds and Fine Jewelry

Q. *How have you glorified God?*
Did hair for twenty-three years and had three of my own salons

Q. *Do you have a soul?*
I washed linens in a Hospital Laundry

Q. *How do you know that you have a soul?*
I worked as a Phlebotomist and
Certified Emergency Medical Technician
for eight years

Q. *What is your soul?*
A Kitchen Manager

Q. *What is sin?*
Director of Housekeeping at a 423-condominium resort
on the beach in Florida

Susan Elizabeth Howe

Q. What will change your heart?
Six years as a Bouncer and Night Auditor
Q. What does God require of you?
Personal Assistant
Front Desk Clerk
Q. How have you repented?
Sold Avon and Tupperware door-to-door
Q. What is election?
I have two sons
Q. What is justification?
One adopted son and one adopted daughter.
Q. What is righteousness?
I miscarried seven times.

Meth Child

Little wanderer who came to earth
in a sand-filled tire in the city park
where your mother gave birth,
how you glow and funk
against the tree-draped dark.
How you whimpered and spit
out the angel dust and weed mist
of your first years. "The dog
will take care of you," your mother
said. When she came back she moaned
like the pipe that seeped into the duck pond
and broke up its skin of sky and sun
and cloud—pictures that taught you
what happened dawn after night
after night. Fourteen now,
you know rashes, blisters, falling,
cold, sometimes food. What
you've learned: right is anything
you want, cruelty everyone
who hurts you—the man who pushed
between your legs until you bled
and the man who held your arms
and locked you in the cop car.
You've been sent to a home

Susan Elizabeth Howe

where people tell you eat, sleep,
learn these marks, they mean things.
You want nuggets and fries,
Pixie Stix, candy rocks. You want
to throw up. You want the jacket with fringe
in the mall. Of course you make friends
with a knife. But only your thighs
belly armpits places no one can see
how you crave to sting and scream
you're here, to make them sorry
when you disappear.

The Last Villager

They said,

> *You made your son a sheep bladder*
> *football. We made him a soldier.*

They said,

> *You wasted goat hair stuffing*
> *your daughter's doll—what wife*
> *needs a doll?*

They said,

> *Deny to the inspectors you lived*
> *here if you want to keep*
>
> *your tongue.*

I kept my tongue.

When they shot us I fell
under bodies too many
above to hear me   breathing   then crawled
from the trench to the road

to find peace keeper, rights worker, doctor, journalist
someone to tell
to commit our names   *Ebele*
                        Dsane
                        Apuri
                        Osadolo

Susan Elizabeth Howe

to a post, a wire, a record on paper, a web, a cloud,
a wave circling the earth,
my wife, my children, me   so others
must know we loved
            the taste of red jujube,
            the click of locusts in long grass.

The whole of us they lost.

    A part of God, we walked home
    each afternoon when late light turned
    grain heads to flames that didn't burn
    our fingers as we brushed them.

III

Americo-Centric

Prayers to Americo-centric Gods

Oh God of Parking,
you who have turned fickle-
ness into metaphysics, won't you
bless my husband and me
with the least space
at this three-hundred-dollar-
a-ticket extravaganza? How
have we sinned that you favor
the Volvo and leave us to search
clogged lots and garages
to the periphery of the inhabited world?

Tattoo God and Beard God, I beg
you, don't fight over my son.
You have the Taliban, great Bearded One,
Hasidic Jews, ZZ Top, yea, even Lincoln.
Holy Tatt, you've covered so much flesh,
purple, orange, and green on Harley
riders, scrolled blue-black NBA player bodies,
not to mention haunch and boob, cheek
and thigh of sexy starlets.
If you must have my son, leave him
to the other member of your trinity,
God of Time-Wasting Electronics.

Susan Elizabeth Howe

Salad God, ding me
in the back of the head
with your garbanzo bean shooter
each time I order a giant caramel
chocolate shake, each time I raise
a pork burrito to my lips. Teach me
the joy of the edamame, ravish me
with the redness of your holy tomato.

Lint God, I fear your gathering power
under the bed. God of Static, don't shock
me, I sacrifice synthetics. Bungee God, carry me off,
spring me back. Tax God, reward
my truthfulness. I bow before you all,
Gods Whose Name is Legion, who goad,
prick, haggle, crack, who swell,
who bide your time, who plan on
fame and fatness going viral.

Selah

Great is the name of my God; his righteousness is as a
Caldera hot tub with hydro-massage jets frothing. His care
is as a biosphere in the desert. Yea, my God is as a soothing
mud bath, a line of warm stones on my back, a full body
Swedish massage. Selah.

He hath protected me from enemies who would defile,
even slay me. My legs were not blown off above the knees
by an IED, nor did an ambush strafe and sting with bullets.
Yea, God hath led me through the mall in safety to buy a
hand-embroidered gray silk skirt and sweater of Mongolian
cashmere. Selah.

Behold the tower, the two great towers did not fall on me.
God hath preserved me in the mountains, with the antler
chandeliers and bison hide sofas of my retreat, yea, rugs of
the polar and the grizzly bear, the Navajo and Hopi, even my
Carrera marble wet bar, my buttered popcorn machine. I will
praise the name of my God day and night. Selah.

He hath kept my enemies from throwing gasoline and lit
matches on me; yea, he hath preserved me to walk in Miu
Miu crisscross calf-hair platform sandals and Giuseppe
Zanotti glitter ballet flats. I will clothe myself in Prada, Vera
Wang, and Gucci for his glory. Selah.

Surely goodness and mercy will follow all the days of my life.
I have dined on pear and goat cheese salad on a bed of baby
greens, macadamia-encrusted halibut with mango salsa, and
chocolate and chipotle mousse topped with French-vanilla
whipped cream. I have put my trust in my God, who will save
me from drought, hurricanes, terrorists, oil spills, all worldly
catastrophes. Selah.

Susan Elizabeth Howe

Questions for the Rain

Why do you stink of worms and slime?

When are you dull, when are you sparkly?

As you descend on flooded towns, Burning Man, the pope's open-air mass, tai-chi, don't you care that you weren't invited?

How did you come upon your infinite disguises?

What color is your shawl—iris? forsythia?

Are you mere element, sheen on which I fling my angst? Or will you talk back?

Do both the just and the unjust emit an electric aura?

Do you quiver before each flash?

What have you not washed away—ash? semen? wanderlust? blood?

Would you rather drown me or a diamondback? A blow snake or a rat?

What was it like, the oblong orbit of the comet?

If I drink nothing but you, can I be forgiven?

Will you soothe my burns, or ache in my scars?

What Dysfunction?

Battered by television news, I
escape to the cabin. But don't go
outside, just close windows
against wind, open them
against heat, dust bones
who knows who brought back
from hikes: three antlers
by the vinegar jug, on the sill
a lizard's needle-thin tail.
Outside, the entire backbone
of a mule deer. Five steer skulls
showed up at the fire pit
three have wandered off.
The last two stare through the window,
their eye sockets accuse me
of avoiding thorny tasks. It's true
I haven't gassed the beetles
that fly down from ceiling planks—
prehistoric creatures or small
packets of truth? The live ones
I carry outside. The dead, I coffin
in a paper towel and gently
proceed to the trash.
Either way they point out
my lethargy, my naps,
the root cause of which I know

Susan Elizabeth Howe

is dread of the demolition derby
of daily American life,
and I'm not the only one
too worn down to watch.
Maybe all the players
should come to the red desert
for rust and rejuvenation. Yes rust.
See if they can do something less
death-inducing: stop cell phone batteries
from failing, stamp out the plastic gun,
capture airborne cottonwood fluff,
consider erosion as a metaphysical
duck in the coal mine, enlist
the capacities of dust.

Rhymes with Oblation

Not being priests or vestal virgins, we seldom speak the word oblation,

as in, Oh, God (or Gods), we have fallen to temptation;

have poisoned reefs, bashed baby seals, harpooned the world's cetaceans;

have warmed the globe and killed the wolves and caused deforestation;

have infected our own livers, brains, genitals, big toes, until they flame in pulsation;

have eaten chicken buckets then fudgy turtle cheesecakes, cleansing with purgation;

while boating have refused to wear devices for flotation;

have drunk beer, stout, mead, ale, wine, gin, vodka, saki, scotch, whiskey, bourbon, cognac, sherry, rum in decades-long inebriation;

have let zombies into art as well as dinner conversation;

have abandoned words (RU my bff—lol), and substituted :) for punctuation;

have made the teenaged body a fixation;

have danced the salsa and electric slide in sexual gyration;

Susan Elizabeth Howe

have Netflixed killer-crusher films to heighten our
sensations;

have feared that Syrians, Mexicans, and probably Canadians
are poised for U.S. invasion;

therefore, Oh God (or Gods), we pour upon the altar this
oblation—

oils of magnolia, sweet alyssum, frangipani, and carnation—

and plant our faces in the most extreme prostration

to beg forgiveness, still believing that we don't deserve
damnation:

the ash-covered survivor's face fills us with elation.

IV

Messengers and Familiars

What Is a Grackle?

A comfort common to Southwest desert
parking lots, a familiar, a messenger,
an overlooked angel oiled by asphalt,

consolation of the casino, supermarket
spiritual guide picking at a free-today
hot dog, a dropped grape or lentil,

its purple-green head iridescent,
its long keel of a tail.
Black birds but not *blackbirds*

with their showy epaulettes blood-red
as a war field. Grackles glint
like lacquered ebony, the females brunhildas,

if by brunhilda you mean "brown-headed,"
not the German "ready for battle." Blind
to centuries of borders, of battles, they waddle

stiff-legged at your feet, a janitorial sweep
to their tails, checking cart tires and light poles
for moths, beetles, singing their seven songs—

slides, whistles, wheezes, catcalls, chirps,
murmurs, clucks—to console you
for your losses: stolen cars, mortgage

payments spun to mist at a roulette table,
the beloved who breathed fire and scorched
your wedding clothes. *Folly and wreckage*

are the lot of life, they mutter, hopping on
the packs of backerboard and spackle.
We've fallen from Mayan temples.

In a past life we prophesied.
In a past life we were gods.

Advice from the Grackle

the seven songs

1.
After joy raises you into the stratosphere,
ride earth's colors as you wheel down.
2.
Fear backs you into a cave,
only then do you cackle and hiss.
3.
Curse at a tornado and it might curse back.
4.
Why kick pebbles on your enemy?
You will die without burying him.
5.
The ascent out of despair
must be steady, slow, or your lungs
will explode, your blood boil.
6.
Which is wisest: to endure hunger
or waddle among wolves?
7.
Warn those you love when the predator
approaches. Screech loudest
if the predator is you.

"Buckle Up With Jesus,"

he says or he won't take me with him on the high
roads and the low roads, the freeways
and the greenways, the paved roads, the gravel,
the dirt. I always said if a heavenly red
Cadillac pulled up in front of me, I'd get in.
"Honey, let me tell you about your Grandpa,"
Jesus says, "my best friend for sixty years.
Hunting ducks in a blind out at the lake,
we made a pact to stay out of the mines."
Mountain Dew all around or whatever
I want in my 44-ounce cup to suck up
the laziness, fatigue, that fibromyalgia disease.
Everyone has a chest tattoo and no work to do.
For kicks I skate the empty Walmart where miners
used to spend their money. Then Jesus hands me
an old flyer that says *Don't wait for that first
job! Work now for Hennessy!* and shows a kid
about ten running the chute, hanging on
by his boots while he dumps the bucket.
"That's Trig," Jesus says, "and there he sits."
We pull up to his porch, the old boy
over fifty and not a Walmart stocker
or meat locker job open in two counties.
Jesus wants Trig to ride up to the lake, punches
the button that puts the top down. "I'm good,"
Trig says. "I don't want no lessons
in how to be." Jesus just hopes to tell him
about his lost love Penelope, the one
with the snake. "What kind, Trig?"
Trig doesn't know but it was three feet long,
with a brownish pinkish paisley pattern. Hers
since it was five days old and she wore it
like a stole around her neck. A lure the old boy
couldn't resist. "Don't call him the old boy,"
Jesus tells me. "Get in back, will you?"

Susan Elizabeth Howe

So I have to unbuckle and move and buckle
again and let Trig take shotgun—Jesus likes
him more than he likes me. "Emmy, are you two
acquainted?" We are, on account of the rink
Trig manages weekends where I'm the fastest
skater in the pack. We drive off, sun on our shoulders,
hair blowing back, and Jesus says, "Emmy, Trig's
always been fond of Penelope and vice versa.
She called her snake Trig so she could think of him
daily. Trig, last March Penny wore your namesnake
under a scarf on a bus to Wheeling to get her Social
Security. She touched it now and then to be sure
it was there, but turned out when she went to get off,
that reptile had skinked itself into thin air. All
the people got out, she called and cooed,
but Trig must have wrapped himself up
inside a seat back or the lighting track. Penny
stayed in Wheeling searching for that snake,
heartbroken, because she'd already lost you."
By now we're up in the dense trees,
the clean smell of pines, and Jesus says, "Trig,
I'm getting a sense of loyalty off you,
a feminine sense, is it the queen of hearts?"
So this is how Jesus works. Then Trig can't wait
to get back to town and buy a bus ticket.
"Sure," Jesus says, "I'll lend you the money,"
so we make a U turn and forget the lake.
But I'm having a ball in the Cadillac,
and all the way down we try out names
for the roller derby team Jesus says
we ought to start—Trig could coach and I
could be the star—Maybe Jugular, or
The Slingers. How about Tungsten?
The Lift? Cold Fusion? Seismic Shift?

Oh, Emily

Why do you appear to me
as a fly
on your grave's black rail?

I've read every poem.
I've taken the tour,
stood in your bedroom, secretly

touched your Indian paisley shawl,
fingered the worn thread
of its fringe. Here,

I pluck a buttercup growing
above your mortal
heart to press in my journal.

You're after the soul—
all souls—bobolink,
bee, volcano, Susan,

Wadsworth, even God—
and look at me
with bulbous

hexagonal eyes that see
at once my stains,
my dithering, my

Susan Elizabeth Howe

hairline cracks. I break
contact, stare at the rainbow
of your name on the headstone,

afraid of disappearing
into your lightning
mind. I disappoint.

But you must know distance
is not indifference. Your poems
with their white buzz cross to me,

settle on my hands, walk
up and down my arms, knock
against my eyes, my brain.

Bulletins from Immortality

"The Only News I know
Is bulletins all day
From Immortality."
—Emily Dickinson

Feathers must be returned to the birds that grew them.
All the feathers. Even the flamingo's. Even the painted
bunting's. Dodo feathers were never authorized for
angelic use.

We have an abundant supply of mustard seeds, pearls,
yeast, nets, vines, grapes, figs, calves, and swine, if you
need them for your parables.

Volunteers needed to exorcise vampires from our
beloved bats. After dinner proceed to the caves.

Meet your progenitors at the tailgate party now taking
place in the Elysian Fields.

The new class in luminosity and hue will help you learn
the complications of your personal emotions. Check
your in-thoughts for the schedule.

Passages between realms are always open, but keep
moving. Traffic stoppages have been horrendous,
especially ingress from the mortal side.

Tip for the day: The best way to influence a beloved
mortal is from within the steam of a delicious soup.

Will Ms. Dickinson report in the next assembly what
she meant by "perchance" in *perchance Eternity*. Her
speculations on our aura and sway?

Potato Lore

Cleave a bluenose
potato, rub a piece on your wart,
plant it and the wart
will vanish
as the potato blooms.

To cure rheumatism
pocket a potato, finger it
daily as it blisters
then shrivels.

So the blow to your face
won't swell,
chop a potato,
mash its tingling
juice on the gathering bruise.

A warm potato in bed
does away with the cramp.

Some cures depend on the potato's
wholeness, the song inside.
Others require breaking open
the heart.

Consider the luminosity
of the rotting potato,
how hope shimmers
above moldering heaps.

And the way to light
an electric bulb: two pennies,
two zinc-plated nails, three
pieces of copper wire,
one large potato.

All Things

With my finger I trace
spirals on the cliff face.
An eye's iris swirls into
the coiled horn of a desert
sheep. Undulant waves
bend like sidewinding snakes
or valleys and hills.
Here the trunk of a man
looks like a womb. Is this
an egg or a bull's-eye?

Echoes, reverberations
I felt as I picked my path
between junipers, creosote
bushes, prickly pear,
path back to this
artist this woman
who drew me
into her vision,

a breath left a millenium
ago, as she crushed her last
pollen for yellow,
paintbrush for red, swirled
them into daubs of sheep fat,
shaped what she needed
to touch me
across this sandstone,
my hand print over
her hand print.

Susan Elizabeth Howe

Petitions to Sulis Minerva from Today's Worshipers

notes dropped into her holy spring

Bluette to the goddess. I give your divinity my Apple 13, pink, ultra-thin. Do not allow sleep or health to whoever has stolen it, whether man or woman whether Pole or Slav or Greek. Only you, dear lady, can retrieve it.

~

Hi Sulis Minerva, this is Annie. Please please please take over for my mother.

~

May he who carried away the lovely Vanessa be obscenely devoured by a school of sharks. I, Elliot, am your petitioner, a worshiper of your fluid charms.

~

Incomparable Sulis Minerva, the investors in the coming luxury mall ask a curse on our competitors. May they lose blood and eyes and every limb and have their intestines eaten away. For your favor, Goddess, and the city council's blessing, we place in your fountain these sixty thousand coins.

~

My queen, my beloved, my one light, I devote myself to your service. Tell me what to do. Jack, barman at the Slug and Lettuce

~

Oh great Sulis Minerva, through some deceit Ralph, the
weasel in accounting, ripped away my promotion. Disfigure
the face of that sneering rodent, make him hideous to
Sarah the vice president, return her attention to my assets.
Remember me, Fabian Cash.

⁓

Whoever stole from Emo the Druid the hundred quid, will
you, Lady Goddess, punish him with fleas and crabs while I
have to feed myself on Picadilly trash?

⁓

I pray, dear lady, for your power, your wiles, and offer this
lavender—it smells strongly of human desire. What words
will teach my child to want, yes, but to wait?

⁓

O Sulis Minerva, whose very name means wisdom, my heart
speaks a different tongue. Please interpret *zzzhhhh* and
again *zzzhhh*. Also *huh-huh-huh-huh*. I, Gabriela Graciela, will
worship at your fountain each day the meaning isn't death.

IV

Stags and Hens

Stags and Hens' Night in Nottingham

A voluntary outing, in no way obligated. Must, as in you must do this, suggests smells and dust, crumbling. On the other hand, let us, untrammeled, carouse in the high street. That American abomination of a burger joint. Pakistani Palace. Maybe Nando's, maybe Callisto's. Local pubs—Owl and Whistle, Hog and Jowl. With a sense of abandon. Women assembled. All the boys—some of my best friends are legally trained.

Outside, if you're not drinking, says the bouncer, the bounder who corrals us at the door. News to him: human animals graze, browse, pee in the alley. This one swore he was vegetarian, then he ate an ostrich chop, then he joined the rave: nine o'clock sharp at the old castle, the meeting point. Of historical evaporation. Of public remorse. Of the slippage of lace.

In no way slipping—hand-made lace. Believe this: dangling crystal over silk leads to an anthropomorphic view of God. Some of my best assets are shoulders, bared. Frigid out here in the square: skin of the inner arm, upper arm, clavicle, neck, gooseflesh. Guinness flesh. If one slips on the ice, if one sees one's breath? Shows one's legs under a skimpy skirt?

Mouths, chests. Aversion, attraction plotted on a graph. See, the line crenelates like a cock's comb. Didn't I meet you in the chip shop? In the back of the yellow cab? My skinny strap, your sequin scratch, biceps, short-cropped beard, whiskey breath. Oh-ho, stags and hens, muster, rally, enlace, mesh!

He was a moose until he became an ape. She was a Rhode Island red until she became a lipid. Some of my best nights called for quires or possibly quills. Gusto smeared on the corned beef, the Cornish pasty. Mustard with that? Unless bangers and mash. Unless all manner of pints. Unless the concert comes off and Jake Bugg headlines Splendour.

Susan Elizabeth Howe

Beauty Treatment

I'm here for the deluxe package—full-body
massage, geyser mudpack, pedicure,
face and hair later, after my kale smoothie.

What languor in the foot bath, *languor*,
with its lolling u, which I follow
through dense vegetation into the Old South,

mint juleps on the verandah; women
rubbing up their gold lace with soda,
vinegar, alcohol, chalk, and ashes;

women like China dolls bleaching
their faces in lemon juice, smoothing
their hair with lard and bear fat pomade

in the hot, moist summer, basting themselves
inside hoop skirts starched and frilled
with flounces, puffs, cords, quillings, ruches.

"Ashley, Ashley, I'm melting,"
but Ashley expects it,
so Scarlett comes back with me

to hang around the Salon and Day Spa
reading *Vogue* and *Elle*,
thrilled to get out of those skirts,

to wait her turn at the wash basin,
admiring the advances—lash extensions,
even an exclusive bird-poop facial.

Cupcake

Hard as nails! Tough as bricks!
We're the class of '66!

Under the parachute lit with twinkle lights
and billowing in the gym we've stuffed
forty years into tuxes and gowns.
Someone insisted on lemonade is it spiked
just like the prom to get us going.
Goat Spencer
wrote a novel for kids.
Merri G. married a deaf cook
then a Nicaraguan actor then a long-haul
trucker they became a team
drove five years coast to coast
without a single room to call home.
Craig Paulsen stole a sheep
graduation night got caught got off
became a prison guard.
Jeff Goss under fire
in Vietnam rescued wounded soldier
after soldier why did he go out
again maybe suicide the bullet fingered
his heart.
Ginny Ash lost him
mourned ten years in a commune
killed her own baby spent her last
years in the state mental no maybe
she didn't die.
Where are
Susan Hassenfritz? the Hansen twins?
Donald and David Klemm? they left
for college and never came back.

Susan Elizabeth Howe

              The old king
of the junior prom won't tell us
his story nor will the queen they're
back in the spotlight dancing
to that sex-sea song their theme
"Ebb Tide." Her above-the-elbow
white gloves and pink dress match
his pink cummerbund and bow tie.
They didn't break up marry someone else
their kids didn't go anorexic wind up
in fast food they aren't bored
with marriage with themselves
their bodies are supple and lithe.
They're still at the '65 junior prom
and later they'll have sex in their clothes
on the back seat of his old GTO
whatever hotel they take for the night.
              Tomorrow Laurel Ostergaard
replaces six knees Kathy Chapman
has to fire an embezzler press charges
Alan Warnick flies back to his accounting
firm in Illinois but the prom queen
and her king will wait by the high school
for their divorces
in the new Nostalgia Bakery
share one red velvet cupcake
specialty of the house.

Knife at the Wedding

Who gave us a weapon?
Precision blade

under the gold foil,
gold ribbon shredded
to curl.

No card with this package.
An enemy? An ex?

High-carbon steel
for boning, cleaving.

Was the giver's point pain?
A specialized hunger?

To be yourself. To cut yourself
out of stone.

Our first stab
at faith, fidelity, sharing a bed.

I bless you, said the priest,
our innocence his thrust.
You will bless each other.

Blesser, French for "to wound."

We take each other by the wrist,
knowing what we do.

We promise.

Susan Elizabeth Howe

The One Time We Met at Midnight

I have somehow revised the pool
to be larger, more—

a perfect blue-lit lagoon
inside a world-class resort—but no,

it was our aging complex's simple
kidney, unheated, chlorinated,
reflecting a few porch lights.

No Lifeguard. Swim at Your Own Risk.

Still, I return there, my arms
on your bare shoulders and you

pulling me through the deep end, swimming
for us both. And then I was on my back
between the moon and the Big Dipper, released

from gravity, and you dived
below me then back up, lifting me
into a bad water ballet moment
until I slipped and splashed.

Floating there, we fit perfectly,
the same coolness in our bodies,
the water, and the air,

below mountains raised eons before,
dark shapes above a valley
longer, deeper

than our lives. We moved forward
and back the length of the pool

through a moment that would extend
into the future because it meant nothing
more than itself. We were never

in love. But I often find myself
sliding through that pool,

not worried about who
might see us as we drifted together

then farther and farther
apart.

Susan Elizabeth Howe

My Sadness

My sadness eats sauerkraut because she's allergic to sauerkraut.

My sadness roams heating ducts, shuffling through the lint.

My sadness sharpens her teeth.

My sadness starts the avalanche she gets caught in.

My sadness wears a crown adorned with plastic rubies and a circlet of rabbit fur.

My sadness weeps over the word *adorned*.

My sadness wanders the fields looking for kildeer nests.

My sadness wades the shallows bare-legged, attracting leeches.

My sadness calls leeches bloodsuckers.

My sadness tries out for the hummingbird then feels inadequate when the meaty tackle gets the part.

My sadness wears her hair down to her tush and irons it.

My sadness, believing sugar to be a thickening agent, ruins the pudding.

My sadness takes up throat-singing and wins a horse.

My sadness shrinks to the size of a salmon egg but never washes away in the current.

VI

Brood

Brood

Follow a wall of fire, two days past.
Smoke in the charred rabbit brush, sticks
of juniper, hot spots under your boots.

Oxycontin, Percocet, codeine, uncontrolled
Demerol got you here, forest service summer job
on the fire lines, your wife & kids

gone to Connecticut, away from the burnout
of your business, your anger, why did she leave?
The path ahead is ash, miserable slick ash

on the mountain, nothing but boulders
to hold you to the slope, your shins scraped,
bloodied, if you slip. Look at that chocolate

chicken ahead, Easter candy left from a hunt,
how did it survive? No, sage grouse
still on her nest. She held her ground,

held and burned. Brooding. She's black
soot that falls through your fingers
as you bend and brush her perfect form

into a shapeless pile. And the chicks
start to peep, still alive and you can crush
that hope, grind it out with your boots

or tuck them into your vest
until you get them to a sanctuary
because now you know their mother's

fierceness and how she kept them alive.

Susan Elizabeth Howe

The Skin of the Story

Three of her children were taken:

one whispered
out of life by a flapping heart,

one stoned in the head by a tumor,

one catapulted through a windshield
into the hereafter.

Unable to pierce God, to fathom
his depths, she bargained for the others:

If you need a life, take mine. Then came

disintegrating veins,
her feet roped,
swollen purple;

the fall in Mexico, no words
to tell the doctor
he set the unbroken leg;

threatened blindness,
the chiseling of her eye sockets;

replacement of her color
by a blankness one
brain cell at a time.

This is the skin of the story
that held her together:

six children prospered.

When she broke her neck
on the stairs
after her last child's wedding,

she believed she had cracked
God's code:
what he meant by
marrow

in the bones.

Susan Elizabeth Howe

There Is No Wing Like Meaning

no meaning like pelicans in flight,
no flight like wind whispering a sandstone arch,
no arch like a beloved's change of heart,
no heart as quick as a mirror's flash,
no flash intricate as lightning's map,
no map detailed as a dragonfly's eye,
no eye like Earth as far galaxy
stars explode in gaseous, limitless wings.

The Cormorant, My Mother

So many mothers.
I learned the scent of mine

shaking off sunlight,
blue-black on the nest tree,

wings spread to dry after harsh
hours fishing for her gangly child.

Match for any predator. Eel, sea snake,
whatever animal threatened

she swallowed and, half-digested,
spewed it into my mouth.

It would have devoured you,
take it as food. I dangled, I slapped,

I learned to follow her eye,
to enter the hunt with as little splash

as a knife, to surprise.
Sun glints on the Long Water.

I wait on a post drying my wings.
Hunger waits on a post

near me. I know it is hunger,
in the glint of the waves I see

my mother slipping,
the fathoms she'll descend

to thwart me. I lift off. My wings flap
and fail. Before I reach the dark

center, she dives.

Susan Elizabeth Howe

I Aspire to the Brightness of the Dark-Eyed Junco

I want a black head, brown back and tail, reddish
wings. I want to feel the tension between flit
and fly. I want to shelter inside conifers
that offer me seeds, heat for star-cold nights.

I want to prefer millet but eat what I find. I want
to feed on the ground, aware but not frightened
of my enemies. I want my enemies to pounce like
cats, gnash like dogs, deadly if not for my eyes,

beautiful and wary, my flight faster than any attack.
I won't mind the bullies—starlings, magpies, crows
pecking out their spite. I want to bounce off
plate glass. I want to be neat and efficient,

the one to stay when the rest fly, to sense danger
as exaggerated, often unreal, a shadow
through a window, wind whipping a branch
like the tail of a cat. I want to be small and prolific,

two clutches of four eggs a year, a lovely
buff or light green speckled with brown.
I want my mate to feed me grasshoppers
or fat crickets he finds. I want my offspring

to gestate quickly—twelve or thirteen days—
and leave the nest two weeks later, independent
and perfectly formed. I want my children
to look and act like me exactly, to stay low,

to hide in roots and under shaggy pfitzers,
to scratch through leaves and grasses
other birds won't bother, to trust common
sunflowers, to hop along the ground.

Hair of the Dog

Not the medieval practice
saving no one
from rabies (cut a few strands
from the dog that bit you,
bandage them into the wound),

nor the hangover cure
(drink more booze).

Not later iterations: neither
the romance novel nor
the Nicaraguan cigar.

I mean Chloë the pug's hair, shed
across our bedspread thick
as icing, layering the carpet,
the back seat of the car.

Soft-coated Chloë, who settles
beside me on the sofa,
chin on my knee.

Loving the dog,
we endure her shedding, light
hair prickling each fabric surface,
yes, navy blue boiled wool,
yes, black cashmere.

Susan Elizabeth Howe

And by extension, I mean
all the stuff

our son left us—chinchilla cage,
seven king-sized cartons
of college texts, terrarium

complete with poison
dart frog.

As he set off towards
New York's musical isles,
he brought us his broken
Harley with its duct-taped seat,
his full set of bar bells, his overgrown
ficus, a whole van of miscellany
we received with affection,

hair of the dog.

VII

Translated

Words to Help Me Escape the Prison of Irony

Aroma, so the cinnamon of
Bread Pudding will swirl through this poem.
Children, who shouldn't be placed in the sentence, "The children are
Drowning."
Embedded nails in
Foreheads, cheeks, torsos, after the pressure cooker bombs exploded.
Ganglia. Nerve centers know when they've been touched.
Heart, an anagram of *Earth*.
Inebriate of air am I, and debauchée of dew.
Jog, a straightforward action, one foot and then the next.
Kite, silk glued over a string and balsa frame, often reaching great heights.
Lung, four letters that want only to breathe.
Mettle, a personal measure of strength, not to be confused with
Nettle, which stings ankle, back, thigh—any bare skin.
Omnivore, to include all classes of eaters.
Porcupines, which, if they fear you, smack you with their
Quills, instead of implying that you are insipid, inelegant.
Recidivism: to once again disdain meaning will
Slam you back in the box.
Troll, as in "I found a nicer troll."
Umber, earth color.
Visitations. After my mother's funeral, a rainbow in a sunny sky.
Want, to care for my husband while he breaks in his new knee.
Xanadu, paradise where we know as we are known and
Yearn for others as for ourselves. To get there,
Zipline down from the mountain top—the exhilarating way in.

Susan Elizabeth Howe

On Cheese

> The poets have been mysteriously silent
> on the subject of cheese.
> —G.K. Chesterton

My question is why, G.K.,
you didn't weigh in on a wheel
yourself, the Cheddar Gorge
magnificent behind you,
a tang teaching your tongue
how curds break from whey
the way words amass
and hold together
as time drains off and the poem
feeds us, savory, sharp.

Not to mention your lack of research.
See James McIntyre, Scot
turned Canadian, whose "Ode
on the Mammoth Cheese Weighing
Over 7,000 Pounds," personifies,
in single-rhyme quatrains, the great
cheese as a monarch with suitors:

> *We have seen the Queen of Cheese,*
> *Laying quietly at your ease,*
> *Gently fanned by evening breeze—*
> *Thy fair form no flies dare seize.*

I admit this is scant poetry,
doggerel composed on the fly
as the cheese went off to town,

not to mention the misuse of lay
when what the cheese did was lie.

Still, you must admit cheese
to be worthy food for a poem,
as well as instructive allegory
on the act of composing.
McIntyre needed the lesson:
for months the wheels brood, cloth-covered,
and mature at Cheddar in caves
as cool as stone icicles.
So a poem should swirl unconscious,
underground, to gain its particular
heft and essence. Horace recommends
waiting eight years to publish.
Only then the reward: stern
Stiltons and bleus, brie
with a startling slap, soft crumbly
Wensleydale swirled with cranberries.

　Susan Elizabeth Howe

Pasta, Translated

to serve for festivals, saint-days, weddings:
    little pies, large little pies,
    sleeve-like things
    big little canes, little cloth
    bundles

for returning to the ancestral home:
    barley, partridge eyes, cock's
    combs, large rags, snails

to honor a birth:
    little beards, little tongues,
    thimbles, twins, ribbons,
    melon, seeds, rice

for male bonding rituals:
    slaps, pens, tubes,
    moustache-like things,
    hoses, rifles

leading to prayer and meditation:
    little ears, little rings, little
    shells, corals

to survive economic collapse:
    crooked ones, peppercorns,
    shoestring-like things,
    corkscrews, wheels

when tempests howl through darkness:
    mouth pockets, half-
    moons, wolf eyes

to enhance a returning peace:
    pillows, butterflies, stars

Gertrude Stein Does The Apocalypse

> "It is lamentable. It is not if there is
> no undertaker."
>
> —Stein

A pock, a lips, a pocket ellipsis, a pocket, a pocket, a
Quirkiness at home, sloughing into half-light.
Select tones flinging themselves at the star cuddle.
A little brown, a rouge and a falling.
This cinder and this, this one, this one, this one, and this
Flourishing, flouring.
Pre and past tenses, swimming, swathing.
The Simian merges, squeezed and tenderly.
O great Kielbasa, fly up, fly up, my avatar,
My crystal, my single fiscal hierarchical.

Susan Elizabeth Howe

Postmodern Colorado

explain the meaning of barn
explain the meaning of house
explain the disposition
of book shop, strip mall, firehouse
i ask the native in the flood zone

the barn is a thoroughfare wherein trailers roil
the house is that slide of douglas fir
book shop, strip mall, firehouse prostrate themselves
before the wooden Indian
in front of God's Country Cowboy Church

the town Niwot has turned
skeptical about walls
brickcementjoistsbeams all the consonants
indifferent to separation

the sign says scour the sky
for nos. 3 and 4
but doors 3, 4, and 5 slant into the mud
and to what pets bicycles vegetables
camisoles folderol
do the numbers attach

i am driving into the road
in the river the river in the road
unmatched asphalt dominoes for giants
game over

chug through
in a dirty boat

as an oil tank swirls
leaving a wake in a lake
a bleed in the feed

of the swimming cattle,
the paddling dogs,
the finny schools of sheep

mold mixed with whiffs
of sewage

the map calls it Elk Meadow
but i claim Floundering Elk Lake
with island: where stands:
a woman on crutches in pajamas
and a sweater that won't zip

her Pekinese gets a bouffant
the helicopter gets a parking ticket
the Arabian stud gets a ride

Susan Elizabeth Howe

The Arch of Marriage

Two columns rise as the builder intends,
destined to be joined—to vault the heavens

and lift the human spirit into light, or perhaps
to carry water through the sky. They yearn

across the space, incline to meet, voussoir
after voussoir rising together, gravity testing

tensions, internal strength, angles. The keystone,
dropped into the last opening, marries them,

an arch perfect as a Roman aqueduct's
or the highest rib of the Chartres cathedral.

All the stresses spread and ease, balanced,
the new structure prepared for bearing

centuries of weight. Like any magnificent
opening, every view through the arch

frames what should be remembered—a green
keen as Irish fields beyond the hill of Cashel,

lushness like the lilies and bougainvillea
outside an Alhambra window, the ache and blessing

storied in a Canterbury panel of jeweled glass:
Mary and Martha in their own home dining

with their dear Jesus on pears, almonds, bitter
herbs, and lamb stew, the meal they have

prepared for him lit by one candle.

All Things Sing Praise

The anteater's tongue licking praise in the tunnels of the termite mound.

The alpaca spitting praise, olé!

Serrano peppers' praise in perspiration.

Plastic praise: the Taj Mahal, a million interlocking Lego blocks.

Draw bridge praise slowly, slowly opening.

Elevator praise crescendoing on the ninetieth floor.

The uplifted pinkie's praise of the saucer.

Praise of the white matter of the cerebellum.

Nervous praise of the nerves.

Praise of the prosthetic standing in for the missing leg.

Single-toned praise of the tuning fork.

Praise of the bikini wax waxing.

Praise of iodine stinging a cut.

Humble praise of the blue spruce chopped down.

Praise snored or snorted by the contented pug.

Cornsilk praise fertilizing each kernel.

Sticky praise of the traveling cockleburr.

The worm's quiet praise eating the earth.

Susan Elizabeth Howe

"Certain Words Persist at the Center of Each Life"

–Jane Hirshfield

Trying to think of mine, I get *Abishag,*
an Old Testament name I must have heard,
then *palindrome*, which I've never tinkered with,
except Anne Sexton's *rat's star* to which I add
spit tips and *spat taps,* meaning nothing.

Don't I have any words at the center of my life?
How can I get to them? *Apricot tocirpa*, no
but *regal lager* works, beer for kings
though I don't drink and alcohol won't trickle
to my center. Rather, my life seems to float

like a minor planet; words spiral close but never hit—
Cless no one knows this word, my husband's name,
or how he touches then circles out and back,
his goodness clear as the brightest stars—Sirius,
Alpha Centauri. Summer nights, lying outside,

I felt the moon pull itself over the mountains—
moon, yes, a constant—valley lights distant,
cars sliding along the highway, occasional buckets
of molten slag dumped at the steel mill
igniting the whole sky, everywhere *presence*,

a word that makes no sense backwards. A distant time,
steel mill long closed. A child, I didn't know
about degraded air, just stillness, time *level*, stretching
both forward and back. Some spring nights
we'd burn apple branches. Their tips spit and flared,

sparks spread like the trill of a *mountain wren*,
as if someone spat "Taps" into the coolness,
song calling everything down: stars,
flickering lights, *breeze* quieting the orchard.

Acknowledgements

Some of the poems in this collection have appeared in the following journals:

15 Bytes Sunday Blog: "Beauty Treatment"
Denver Quarterly: "Gertrude Stein Does the Apocalype"
Plume Anthology of Poetry: "Selah"
Poetry: "What is a Grackle?" and "Advice from the Grackle"
River Styx: "The Last Villager"

SUSAN ELIZABETH HOWE received a B.A. from Brigham Young University, an M.A. from the University of Utah, and a Ph.D. from the University of Denver. She was a faculty member of the BYU English Department until her retirement in 2016. She has published two previous collections of poetry—*Stone Spirits* and *Salt*—and her poems have appeared in *The New Yorker*, *Poetry*, *Shenandoah*, *Atlanta Review*, *Western Humanities Review*, and many other journals. She has served as a board member and president of the Association for Mormon Letters; contributing editor of *Tar River Poetry*; poetry editor of *Dialogue: A Journal of Mormon Thought*; poetry editor of *Literature and Belief*; managing editor of the *Denver Quarterly*; the editor of *Exponent II*; and a board member of the Utah Humanities Council. She received the 2017 Lifetime Achievement Award of the Association for Mormon Letters. She is currently the associate editor of *BYU Studies Journal*. She lives with her husband Cless Young in Ephraim, Utah.

Made in the USA
Las Vegas, NV
19 May 2023

72267108R00055